Preparing the Unit

1. Visit your school library and local public library to collect an assortment of books about food and farming. The bibliography on the inside front cover suggests some titles you might enjoy.

2. Plan for one or more field trips. Do some checking to find out if there is a farm your students might be able to visit. Other possibilities include a dairy, vineyard, or orchard. Plan to visit a local market. If possible, plan your visit for a time of day when fresh food products are being delivered.

3. Contact the U.S. Department of Agriculture to find out what materials might be available to you at little or no cost.

4. Find community members who might be able to come and speak to your class. These could include farmers, grocers, or anyone who is involved with food products of any kind.

5. Ask the cafeteria manager at your school if you may bring your class to watch deliveries being made and food being prepared. Ask her/him to explain how the food is ordered and where it comes from.

6. Explore your campus to find out if there is an area where your class may plant a garden. If you do not have any available areas, try to round up donations of large planters and potting soil to place in a sunny area outside your classroom.

7. This is a perfect time to bring some animals into the classroom! Incubate some chicken eggs or bring a chicken into the classroom as a pet. They are easy to care for, but the cage must be cleaned daily to keep odor under control! This effort is well worthwhile if students get a chance to see egg production right before their eyes. A feed or animal supply store in your area might be willing to "loan" you a hen for a couple of weeks.

8. Try to find a beekeeper who can come in and discuss the production of honey with your class.

Room Environment

Bulletin Board

Materials for each student:

- 9" x 9" (23 x 23 cm)
  piece of construction paper
- crayons

Steps to follow:

1. Brainstorm and list food products grown on a farm. This can be a plant or animal product.
2. Ask each student to choose one product from the list to draw.
3. Assemble the squares onto a bulletin board to resemble a quilt.
4. Label the bulletin board *Food from the Farm.*

Table Top Farm

This area can be created as a full-class project, or can be a center where students work independently.

Materials:

- green, brown, and blue butcher or construction paper
- scraps of construction paper
- plasticine or modeling clay
- small boxes
- pieces of cardboard
- paint
- pipe cleaners, Popsicle® sticks, twigs
- glue

Steps to follow:

1. Set up a table in your classroom. Cover it with green and brown construction or butcher paper to resemble areas of grass or pasture and plowed areas. Add a blue paper pond.

2. Provide materials listed above for students to make into farm buildings, fences, and trees. Farm animals can be made of clay, or you may wish to use small plastic animals.

3. Post pictures of farms and books about farm life near this display so that they can be used as references.

Livestock for Your Classroom

Turn your classroom into a farm! Use these farm animals to decorate your classroom. They can be taped to the ends of tables, along bookshelves, on chairbacks, or directly to the wall. If time permits, enlarge and cut out enough shapes for each student to paint and stuff one animal. In this way you can create a lively batch of "livestock" for your farm.

Materials:

- animal patterns on the picture cards (pages 14–16).
- newspaper
- paint
- butcher paper
- stapler

Steps to follow:

1. Using an opaque projector, enlarge the animal patterns and trace onto butcher paper.

2. Cut out two of each animal shape.

3. Place the shapes on newspaper, mirror image fashion, and paint.

4. When the paint is dry, staple the edges of the two painted pieces together, painted sides out. Leave open a space about 10 (25.4 cm) inches long.

5. Through the opening, slide crumpled newspaper to fill animal's body.

6. When animal is "plump," staple opening closed.

Farm to Table

Background Information Pages

The following pages (5-9) contain information that will help you provide your students with a basic understanding of how and where food is produced. These pages can be reproduced and bound into a construction paper cover to make a reference booklet, or can be displayed on an overhead projector and used as the basis of a class discussion.

The pages also lend themselves to extended activities, such as those suggested below.

Extensions

1. After reading and discussing this page, ask students to write a sentence or short paragraph beginning with the phrase "Farms are important because _____."

2. Divide students into groups of three or four students. Give each group a sheet of poster paper and paints or markers. Ask each group to create a poster illustrating some activities that might be seen on a farm. Allow time for each group to present these posters to the rest of the class.

3. Use magazine pictures and newspaper ads to create charts or booklets of products grown on the various types of farms mentioned on pages 6–9.

4. Use magazine pictures and newspaper ads to create charts or booklets showing a crop as it is grown and the food product after it has been processed (e.g., an apple, a bottle of apple juice; a cow, an ice cream bar).

5. Use the posters to discover and discuss the faraway places that some foods come from. See the inside back cover for detailed teaching ideas.

What Is a Farm?

A farm is a place where the plants and animals used for food are grown. Most of the food we eat is grown on farms.

In the past almost all families lived on their own little farms. They worked hard to grow enough food for themselves to eat. Now there are fewer farms, but they are large. Farmers use big machinery to help them grow enough food for many people to eat.

Some farms are small.

Some farms are large.

 From Farm to Table EMC 551

Farms Around the World

There are farms of many different sizes all over the world.
The foods that are grown on the large farms are loaded onto trucks, trains, and ships to be sent around the world. All the food on our grocery store shelves traveled from some kind of farm somewhere in the world.

Farming rice in Southeast Asia

Growing bananas in South America

An apple farm in Washington, U.S.A.

Growing corn in Nebraska, U.S.A.

6 From Farm to Table EMC 551

Different Kinds of Crops

The plant products grown on a farm, such as corn and peanuts, are called crops. Some farms specialize in just one kind of crop.

Grain farms grow grain used to make bread and cereal.

Fruit farms have orchards that produce many kinds of fruits.

A vegetable farm might grow lettuce, broccoli, carrots, or many other vegetables.

From Farm to Table EMC 551

Different Kinds of Livestock

Animals raised on a farm, such as cows, chicken, and pigs, are called livestock. Farms that raise cattle and sheep are usually called ranches.

Dairy farms raise cows for their milk.

Chickens are raised for meat and for their eggs.

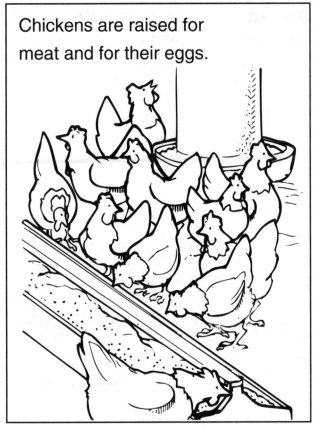

Beef cattle and pigs are raised for their meat.

Doing Work on the Farm

Large farms today depend on modern machinery to plow the fields, plant, and to harvest most crops. Even egg gathering and milking is done by machines.

Some crops, such as many fruits and vegetables, are easily damaged and must be harvested by hand.

Tractors make it possible to plow a lot of land.

This field of wheat is being harvested by machines.

Strawberries are a fruit that must be picked by hand.

Down on the Farm

Down on the farm
When the sun comes up
You hear the rooster crowing.

Down on the farm
When the sun comes up
You hear the rooster crowing.
You see the corn growing.

Down on the farm
When the sun comes up
You hear the rooster crowing.
You see the corn growing.
You smell the cows and horses.

Down on the farm
When the sun comes up
You hear the rooster crowing.
You see the corn growing.
You smell the cows and horses.
You taste a crunchy apple.

Down on the farm
When the sun comes up
You hear the rooster crowing.
You see the corn growing.
You smell the cows and horses.
You taste a crunchy apple.
You pet the woolly sheep.

Down on the farm
When the sun comes up.

Martha Cheney and Diane Hoche Bockwoldt

From Farm to Table EMC 551

Farmer Hats

Materials needed for each student:

- two sheets of large newsprint
- glue
- markers
- crayons
- paint
- masking tape
- colored paper, crepe paper, tissue paper (optional)

Steps to follow:

1. Sandwich two sheets of newsprint together with a thin layer of glue.

2. While the glue is still wet, center the newsprint paper on the child's head and mold to fit.

3. Use the masking tape to hold the shape of the hat.

4. Let hat dry completely.

5. When dry, cut a circular shape for the brim of the hat.

6. Allow students to use markers, crayons, paint, etc., to decorate their hats.

7. Colored paper, crepe paper, etc., can be used to create flowers, hat bands, or other decorations.

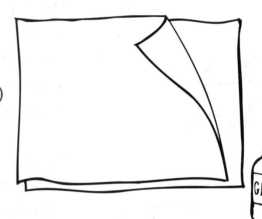

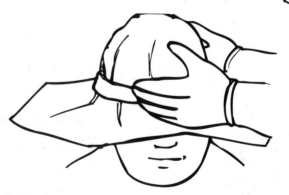

Note: Have each student complete this page by (1) drawing a picture of a person, animal or thing that is useful on a farm and (2) using the lines at the bottom of the page to write a short paragraph about their picture. Cut out and assemble into a class book.

I am _____

_____

My job on the farm is to _____

_____

_____

_____

_____

_____

Picture Card Activities

The picture cards on pages 14-16 can be used as a basis for learning activities in several curriculum areas.

Acrostic Poems

Direct students to choose one of the animals from the set of picture cards. That animal's name will be written vertically down the middle of a piece of lined paper, with one letter on each line. Students will then work to think of words that describe the animal they have chosen. They must come up with a word or phrase that contains each letter in the animal's name. These words are then written across the name of the animal, creating a poem.

Music/Drama

Ask students to color and cut out one of each animal shape. Mount on tongue depressors or strips of tag board to create simple puppets. Sing "Old MacDonald Had a Farm." Allow six students to lead the singing, each holding up the puppet that matches each verse.

Animal Babies

Direct students to draw a baby animal to accompany each of the animals shown in the picture cards. Older students can research to find the names of each baby animal. For younger students, write the names on the board and ask them to match the names of the babies and the adults.

As an added challenge, list additional animals and do research to find the names of their babies.

Note: Reproduce the picture cards to go with activities on page 13.

Picture Cards

From Farm to Table EMC 551

Note: Reproduce the picture cards to go with activities on page 13.

Note: Reproduce the picture cards to go with activities on page 13.

Butter Me Up
Make butter with your students!

Materials needed for each group of four students:

- pint to quart-sized glass jar (with lid)
- 8 oz. (240 ml) carton of whipping cream
- crackers or bread to spread the butter on
- salt
- a bowl
- a child-safe knife for spreading

Steps to follow:

1. Direct students to pour the whipping cream into the jar.

2. Have students close the lid tightly.

3. Have students take turns shaking the jar vigorously.

4. After a few minutes a lump should appear. This is the butter!

5. When butter is formed, have students empty the jar into a bowl. Pour off the liquid and rinse the butter with water.

6. Add a few sprinkles of salt.

7. Allow students to spread the butter onto the bread or crackers. Eat!

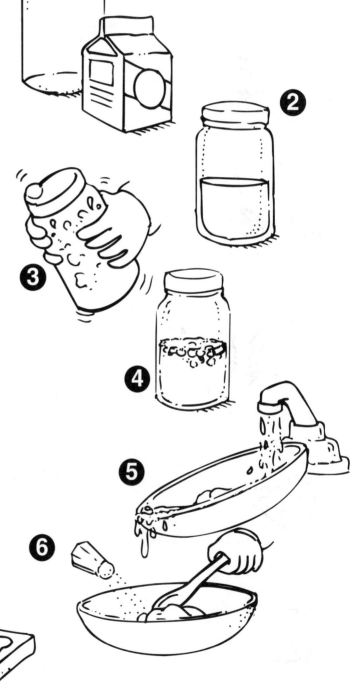

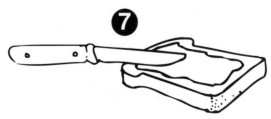

How Seeds Grow

Lima Beans in a Bag

This experiment will give students an insight on how seeds germinate and grow into plants.

Materials needed for each student:

- three dry lima beans
- paper towel
- small self-locking bag
- water

Steps to follow:

1. Have students fold paper towel into quarters and wet it.
2. Place paper towel into small self-locking bag.
3. Have students evenly space three lima beans on top of the wet paper towel.
4. Seal bag.
5. Place bags in a sunny location and watch the beans grow.

Observe and Record

Reproduce the booklet provided below and on the following page for each student. You may want to include more than four pages. Cut apart the pages of the books on the dotted lines and staple them together to form a booklet. Students are to check their beans daily, recording observations if there are changes. Have them use both words and pictures to describe what they see.

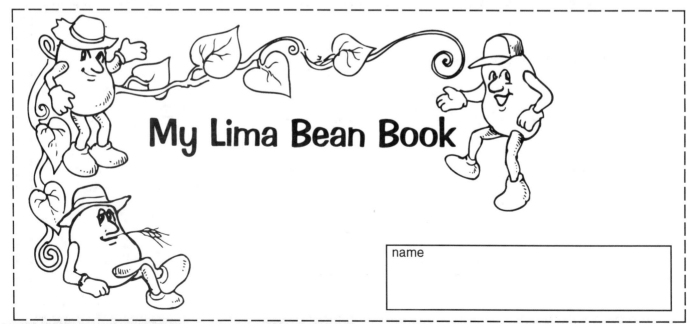

name

What I observed on (date) _____

_____

_____

_____

_____

Draw a picture here.

What I observed on (date) _____

_____

_____

_____

_____

Draw a picture here.

What I observed on (date) _____

_____

_____

_____

_____

Draw a picture here.

Using Literature

> ## *Make Me a Peanut Butter Sandwich and a Glass of Milk*
> by Ken Robbins
> Scholastic, 1992

This is a terrific book that guides students through the real process by which the components of one of their favorite meals is produced. The illustrations are photographs taken throughout the production of bread, peanut butter, and milk. Many of the activities that follow can be used with or without the book, but it does make an excellent springboard.

Motivation

Provide (or ask the students to bring in) bread, peanut butter, and milk. You will also need safe knives for spreading and small paper cups. Also provide a paper napkin for each student. Make and serve peanut butter sandwiches and milk as a snack.

Finding Out What We Know

After the class has finished eating, talk about the components of the snack. Where did the peanut butter come from? The bread? The milk? Chart the ideas that the students come up with. List all ideas, even if they are incorrect.

Reading the Selection

Read the book to your students, in small groups if possible, so that all can see the pictures. Take time to discuss what is happening on each page. It may be necessary with very young children to read and discuss only one portion of the book at one sitting.

Adding New Information

When all students have had a chance to read and discuss the book in small groups, hold a whole-class discussion. Refer back to the chart made earlier. Create a new chart, adding and correcting information from the previous chart.

If you do not have access to *Make Me a Peanut Butter Sandwich and a Glass of Milk*, enlarge the appropriate pages from the student booklet on pages 22-31 or show them on an overhead projector.

Where Does It Come From		
peanut butter	bread	milk
peanut plants	wheat	dairy cows
Georgia	South Dakota	farms

A Fold-Out Book

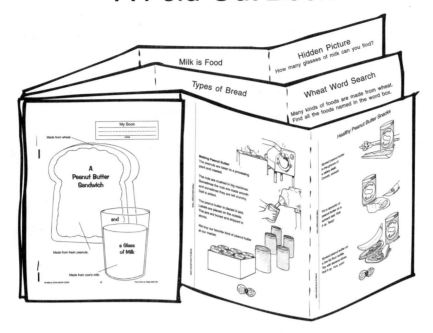

On pages 22-31 you will find a reproducible book for your students to assemble and read. The book consists of three accordion-folded chapters. The production process of peanut butter, bread, and milk is explained and followed by student activity pages.

Each page has a numbered picture key (peanut, slice of bread, milk glass) to help children assemble their books in the correct order.

Decide if you want to discuss and work on the pages before or after the book is assembled.

Materials needed for each student:

- a copy of pages 22-31
- a plain sheet of paper for the back cover
- glue sticks
- stapler
- crayons for coloring the pictures if desired

Steps to follow:

1. Have students lay out the three pages of each chapter in the correct order.

2. Glue the pages together as indicated. Younger groups may need to do this in small groups with adult assistance.

3. Staple the front and back covers as well as the first page of each chapter together.

4. Fold the pages of each chapter to fit within the covers.

My Book

_____

name

Made from wheat.

A Peanut Butter Sandwich

and

a Glass of Milk

Made from fresh peanuts.

Made from cow's milk.

From Farm to Table EMC 551

How Peanut Butter Is Made

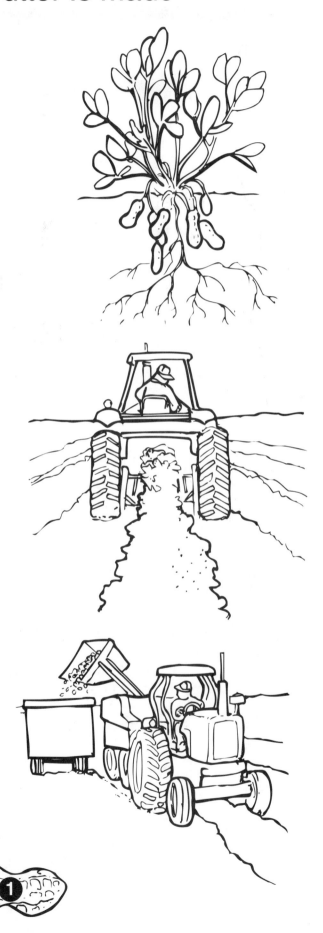

Growing Peanuts

Does it surprise you to learn that peanuts grow underground? In some countries they are called groundnuts. But peanuts are not really nuts. They belong to the same plant family as peas. The part we eat are the seeds of the peanut plant.

The peanut plant grows leaves and flowers like most plants. After the flowers die, stalk-like "pegs" form. The pegs reach into the ground. The ends of the pegs form pods. These pods contain the seeds. After the seeds ripen, the peanuts are dug out of the soil.

Harvesting Peanuts

The peanut plants are dug up when the nuts are ripe. A digger-shaker tractor digs up the plants and lays them in the field.

A combine picks and separates the peanuts from the plants.

1

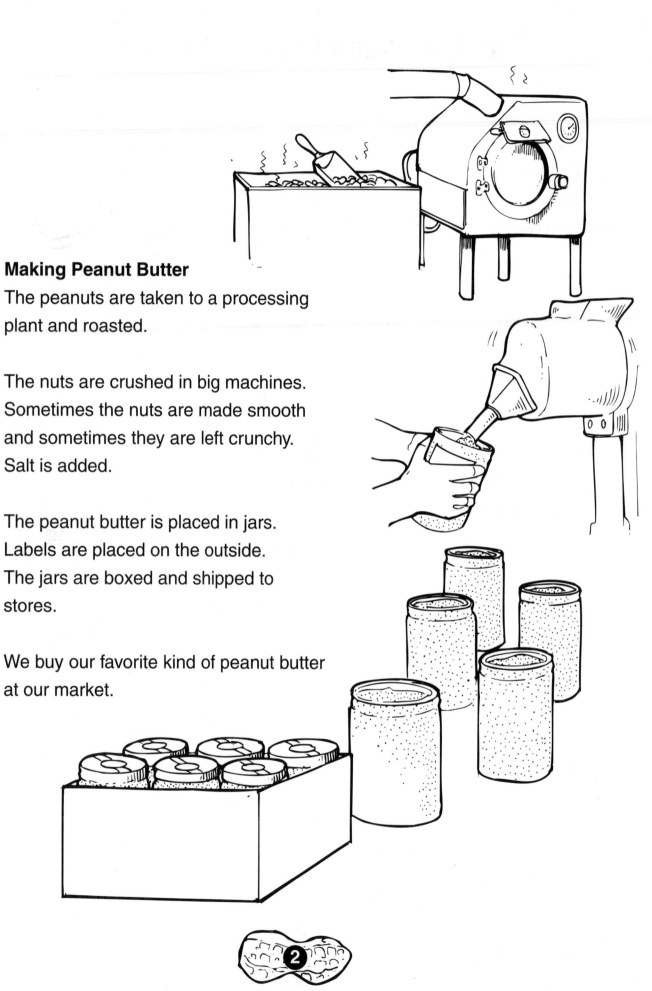

Making Peanut Butter

The peanuts are taken to a processing plant and roasted.

The nuts are crushed in big machines. Sometimes the nuts are made smooth and sometimes they are left crunchy. Salt is added.

The peanut butter is placed in jars. Labels are placed on the outside. The jars are boxed and shipped to stores.

We buy our favorite kind of peanut butter at our market.

2

bes your
ome from?

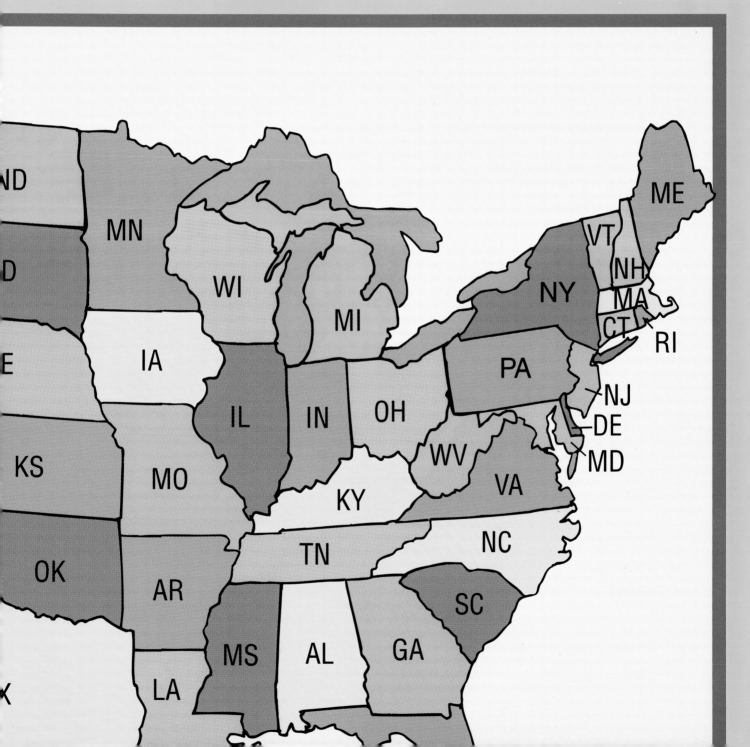

FL

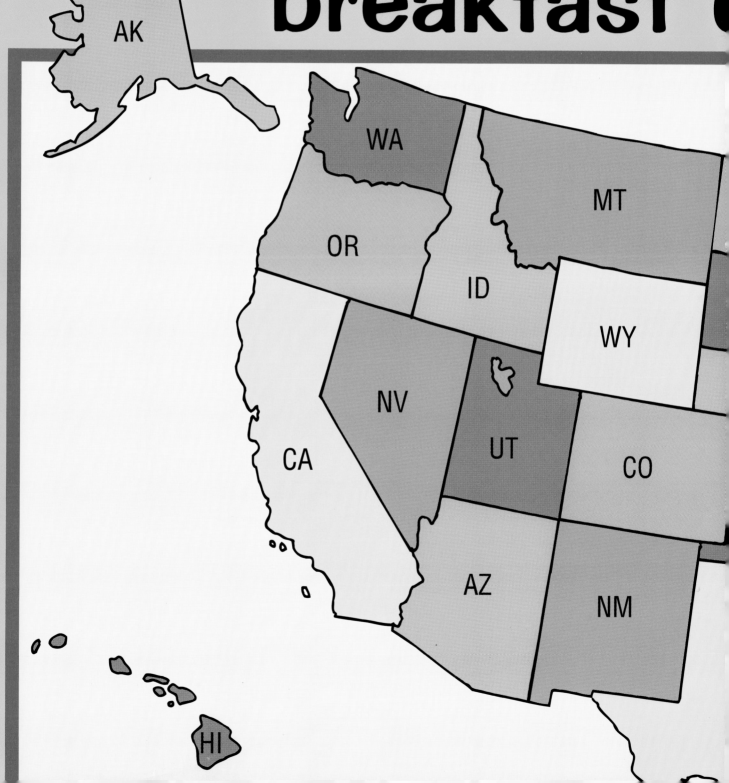

Where d

breakfast c

Africa

Australia

Grapes   Coffee beans   Bananas   Oranges   Pineapple   Wheat   Dairy cattle   Tea   Potatoes

A World of Flavor

South America

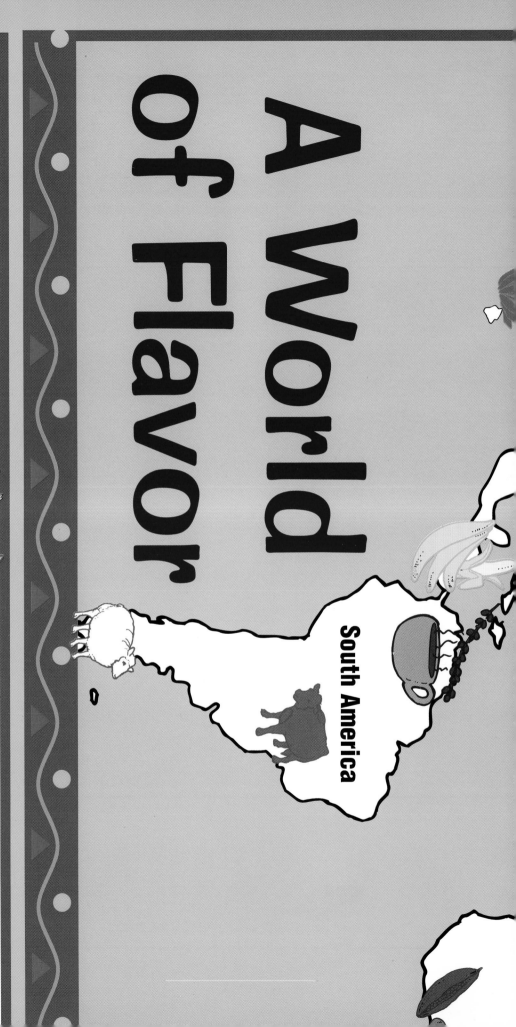

	Kiwi	
	Sheep	
	Beef cattle	
	Coconuts	
	Rice	
	Fish	
	Sugar cane	
	Peanuts	
	Cocoa beans	

Healthy Peanut Butter Snacks

Spread peanut butter
in the groove of
a celery stalk.
Crunch, crunch!

Put a spoonful of
peanut butter on a
spinach leaf. Roll
it up. Tasty!

Spread peanut butter on
a low-fat flour tortilla.
Top with banana slices.
Roll it up. Yum, yum!

3

How Bread Is Made

Bread is made from grain. Wheat is a popular grain used in making bread.

Wheat seeds are planted in a field.
The farmer cares for the plants as they grow.

When the wheat has turned a golden color, a combine cuts it and separates the wheat kernels from the stalks.

The wheat kernels are loaded on a truck and taken to a mill. The mill grinds the kernels into flour. The flour is placed in bags and sent by truck to a bread factory.

The flour is mixed with other ingredients to make bread. It is baked to a golden brown.

We enjoy the bread every day.

1

Types of Bread

Look at these breads that are eaten around the world.
Circle the ones you have eaten.

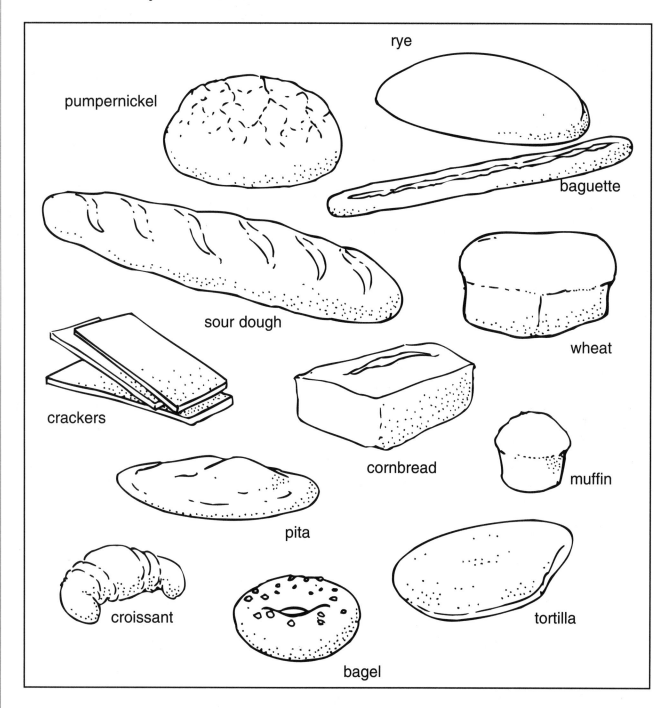

rye

pumpernickel

baguette

sour dough

wheat

crackers

cornbread

muffin

pita

croissant

bagel

tortilla

2

Wheat Word Search

Many kinds of foods are made from wheat.
Find all the foods named in the word box.

```
m u f f i n c e r e a l
u d o u g n p a b a s t
c o o k i e r a i s b o
r u s c u i e n s o r r
a g o l a t t o c t e b
c h n u t k z t u z a r
k n o o d l e s i e d e
e u o c e r l i t z e c
r t o r t i l l a c a k
```

Word Box

biscuit	cookie	noodles
bread	cracker	pasta
cake	doughnut	pretzel
cereal	muffin	tortilla

3

How Milk Is Produced

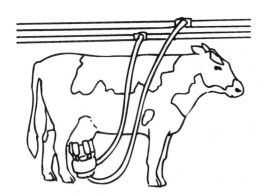

The dairy farmer milks the cows.

The milk is placed in a tanker truck and taken to the dairy.

The milk is heated to kill any germs.

Then the milk is cooled and placed in cartons.

A truck delivers the milk to the grocery store.

We buy the kind of milk we like to drink.

Milk Is Food

Draw four foods made from milk. Tell about them.

Hidden Picture

How many glasses of milk can you find?_____

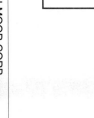

Peanut Butter

(Sung to the tune of "Darlin' Clementine")

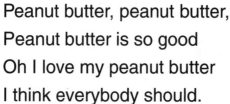
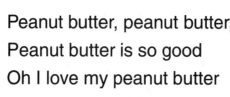

Peanut butter, peanut butter,
Peanut butter is so good
Oh I love my peanut butter
I think everybody should.

Plant the peanuts, plant the peanuts,
Plant the peanuts in the ground
Let them grow until the peanuts
Fill the shell up nice and round.

Roast the peanuts, roast the peanuts,
Roast the peanuts in the shells
When they're done just crack them open
You will really like the smell.

Smash the peanuts, smash the peanuts,
Smash the peanuts to a paste
Now you've made some peanut butter
Go ahead and have a taste.

Martha Cheney and Diane Hoche Bockwoldt

Extension:

As a class, make up a song about other favorite foods. The song should include information about how the food is grown or processed.

Math Explorations and Activities

Milk Carton Math

To provide practice in any type of math computation, set up a bulletin board with various containers from milk products such as yogurt, cottage cheese, whipping cream, sour cream, white and chocolate milks. Wash these containers and pin them to the bulletin board. Into each container, slip numbered index cards on which you have written a particular type of math problem (i.e., the yogurt container might have two digit addition, while the chocolate milk carton features basic multiplication facts). You can tailor the problems to fit the needs of your class. Then, assign students to work a certain number of problems from each container, or all of the problems from a single container, according to individual needs.

Newspaper Numbers

Use the weekly grocery ads from your local newspaper as a basis for some math practice. The activities will vary along with the ability level of your students. Students can be asked to select (or draw) the appropriate coins needed to purchase particular items from the ad. Older students might be asked to determine the total cost of several grocery items. The possibilities are endless. Save several grocery ads and laminate them for durability.

Popcorn Problems

Divide your class into small groups. Give each group 1/4 cup (60 ml) of unpopped popcorn in a paper cup. Ask each group to estimate the number of kernels of corn it has. Give each group a record sheet such as the one shown. Allow someone from each group to report to the class. Pop and eat the popcorn!

From Farm to Table EMC 551

Milk...Keep It Cool

Everyone knows that milk must be kept cold to stay fresh. Do your students know why? It's because milk contains bacteria which grow more slowly under refrigeration. The milk we drink is pasteurized (the process of heating milk to a high temperature) to remove the harmful bacteria. Milk is transported in refrigerated trucks and stored in refrigerated areas.

Exploration

Try this simple experiment with your class to demonstrate why refrigeration is important.

Materials needed for demonstration:
- two equal amounts of fresh milk in separate containers
- a copy of the log on page 35 provided for each student

Discuss the information at the top of the page with your class. Ask questions such as:

Where is milk stored in your home?
Do you think it needs to be refrigerated?
What would happen to the milk if it were not refrigerated?

Directions:

1. Show your students the two containers of milk. Allow enough time for all of your students to observe and smell the milk.

2. Label the two containers of milk - *Refrigerated, Not Refrigerated.*

3. Place one of the containers in a refrigerator and the other in a place in your classroom where it will not be disturbed.

4. Set aside time each day (for three consecutive days) for your students to observe and compare the two containers of milk.

5. Ask your students to record their observations on the *Milk...Keep It Cool* log provided.

Milk...Keep It Cool!

Day	How it Looks		How it Smells	
	Refrigerated	Not Refrigerated	Refrigerated	Not Refrigerated
1				
2				
3				

From Farm to Table EMC 551

The Life of a Loaf

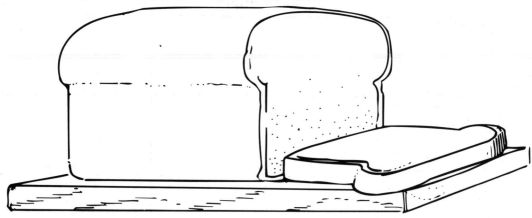

Bread is delivered to stores often because it has a short shelf life. Try this simple experiment with your students to demonstrate that bread spoils easily. Your students will discover what will happen to bread that is not consumed in a few days. As you set up the experiment, ask questions such as:

What happens to bread that is not used in a few days?

Where is your bread stored at home?

Materials needed:

- two slices of bread
- two clear plastic bags
- two paper plates

Have students predict what changes will occur with each slice of bread.

Steps to follow:

1. Place one slice of bread in a plastic bag and close it tightly.

2. Place the other slice of bread in a plastic bag and leave it open.

3. Place each bag on a paper plate.

4. Have your students look at the slices of bread and compare them each day for a two-week period.

5. Ask your students to record their observations on the log provided on page 37.

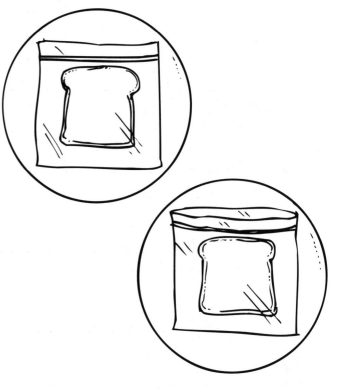

The Life of a Loaf

Day	Sealed Bread	Unsealed Bread
Monday		
Tuesday		
Wednesday		
Thursday		
Friday		

The Life of a Loaf

Day	Sealed Bread	Unsealed Bread
Monday		
Tuesday		
Wednesday		
Thursday		
Friday		

Note: This dramatic presentation traces the story of a small kernel of corn from planting through harvest and processing into a number of corn products.

The Story of Corn
A Play

Characters - Main Speaking Parts

• Corny   • Farmer Fred   • Tiny Cornstalks   • Big Cornstalks

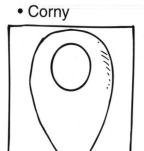 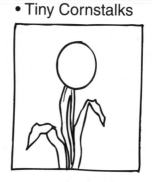  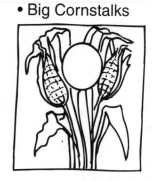

Materials:

- poster board
- paint, markers, or crayons
- scissors

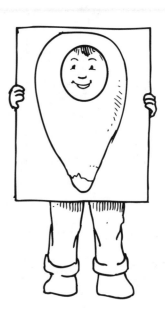

Steps to follow:

1. Form the face hole by tracing around a small plate. Cut out the circle.
2. On each sheet of poster board draw an outline of the "character" you are creating. Make it fill the poster board as much as possible.
3. Paint or color.

Parade of Products Costumes

Students carry construction paper or tagboard signs.
Draw the product or attach an actual package to the sign.

• Popcorn   • Cornbread   • Chicken feed   • Tortillas   • Cereal

   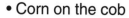 

• Corn on the cob   • Cattle feed   • Corn chips   • Grits   • Corn oil

   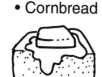

Staging

Main characters can all be on stage, with each character or group coming forward to speak. The Parade of Corn Products comes marching through, and each one shouts out his/ her name and takes a bow at the center of the "stage" area. They remain on stage in rear.)

       From Farm to Table EMC 551

The Story of Corn

Corny: Good morning! I am Cornelius (Cornelia), a friendly little kernel of corn. Just call me Corny. All my friends do! I have been asked to come here today to tell you a little bit about the life of a corn kernel. And what a story it is! It's a story with many different endings...but I guess I'm getting ahead of myself. Let's start with the beginning.

Farmer Fred: This is where I come in. I'm Farmer Fred. I plant thousands and thousands of kernels of corn in my fields every spring.

Tiny Cornstalks: The kernels of corn sprout into tiny cornstalks. That's us! We grow and grow so fast, especially if we get enough rain and sun. Some people say that if you stand in the middle of a cornfield and listen very carefully, you can hear the corn grow!

Big Cornstalks: It must be true, because by late summer, we have grown very big and tall and we have formed a lot of ears. You only have two ears, but we have many!

Corny: This is where it really gets exciting! When the ears of corn are full and ready, a gigantic machine called a combine cuts down the stalks and separates the corn from the cobs.

Farmer Fred: The thousands of kernels I planted have now become millions of kernels!

Corny: And where do they go? They become a parade of corn products for people and animals to eat! Here come some of them now.

(Parade of Corn Products)

Corny: What a parade! Did you know that corn was so amazing? Just look at what those little kernels can do when they put their minds to it!

Tiny Cornstalks: Corn is delicious!

Big Cornstalks: Corn is nutritious!

Corn Products Parade: Corn can be made into lots and lots of products!

Farmer Fred: Corn is wonderful! But, Corny, I think we had better get back to the farm. Those folks out there look hungry, so we need to get to work.

All: Goodbye everybody!

(All exit. Corny stops to speak to the audience one last time.)

Corny: See ya soon in your cereal bowl! *(with a wink)*

Crazy Corn

Make a mosaic with corn products. If possible, display an ear of corn and pictures of corn growing in fields. Discuss how many food products are made from corn. Show students the food materials to be used for the mosaic and allow them to examine and taste materials.

Materials needed for each student:

- popcorn (popped and unpopped)
- cornmeal
- grits
- cereals made from corn such as Kix®, Corn Flakes®, Corn Chex®
- 9" x 12" (23 x 30.5 cm) sheet of chip board or tagboard
- glue

Steps to follow:

1. Have students squeeze glue onto the chip board into a design.
2. Instruct them to work on a small area at a time.
3. Place the corn products on the area of glue to create a mosaic.
4. Let dry completely before displaying.

Fantasy Fruit

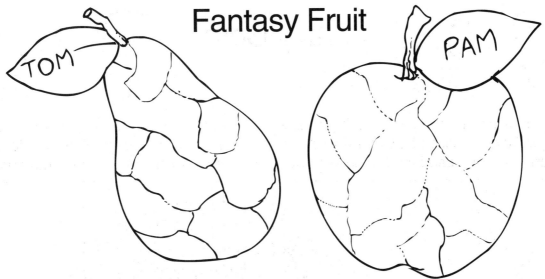

Materials needed for each student:

- aluminum foil
- colored tissue paper, cut into 2" x 2" (5 x 5 cm) squares
- white glue, thinned with water (equal parts)
- paint brush
- small twigs

Steps to follow:

1. Instruct students to loosely crumple and mold aluminum foil into the shape of any fruit. (Fruit should be about the size of child's fist or a little larger.)

   If desired, insert a small twig into the appropriate end of the foil fruit as a stem.

2. Dip paintbrush into glue and use this to paint over a square of tissue laid against foil fruit. Continue layering by painting glue mixture over tissue squares until fruit is completely covered and smooth. Allow to dry on waxed paper.

3. Cut leaves from green construction paper. Write each student's name on a leaf and attach it to their fruit.

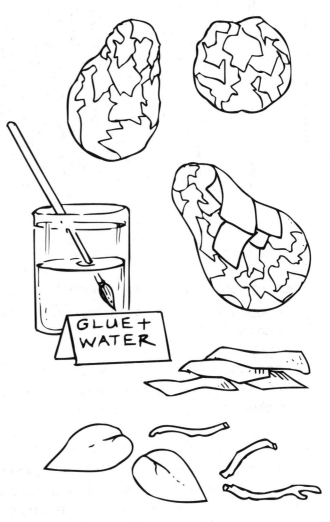

Extension

If desired, students can make several pieces of fruit as holiday gift for parents.

Hilltop Farm

Create Math Word Problems

Tell your students that they are going to go on an imaginary field trip to Hilltop Farm. Brainstorm together and make a list of the kinds of animals they might see. Give students a few sample story problems involving the animals on the list. (There are examples given below for a variety of grade levels.) Then ask students, working independently or in small groups, to create their own story problems. These can be displayed as an interactive bulletin board, or students can swap problems to solve.

 There are four horses on Hilltop Farm. Two of them are in the pasture and the rest are in the barn. How many horses are in the barn?

 Henrietta and Hazel are two speckled hens from Hilltop Farm. Each of them lays one egg every day. How many eggs will the two of them lay in one week?

 Portia had twelve piglets. Pansy had three less. How many piglets did Pansy have?

 There are six geese swimming on the pond. Each goose has seven goslings. How many goslings are there all together?

 Farmer Ferguson has three pastures for his cows to graze in. He has 27 cows. He wants to put an equal number of cows in each pasture. How many cows will be in each pasture?

 Bertha gave two gallons of milk on Monday. Bessie gave half as much. How much milk did Bessie give?

Going Bananas

Bananas, bananas, I buy them at the store.
Bananas, bananas, they come from Ecuador.
Ecuador is tropical, the weather there is hot.
Bananas like to grow there, because it rains a lot.

Bananas on plantations grow in a big green bunch.
The workers cut them off the stems; it makes a great big crunch.
The bunches at the packing plant are washed and packed away.
They're loaded into ships and trucks to travel many days.

The trucks bring some bananas down to the corner store.
They took two weeks to get here or just a little more.
Bananas, bananas, I buy them at the store.
Bananas, bananas, I always want some more.

Martha Cheney and Diane Hoche Bockwoldt

From Farm to Table EMC 551

Growing a Salad

Bring the farm home.
Have your students grow their own food!

Planting and Growing the Salad

Materials for each student:

- a variety of leaf lettuce and radish seeds
- two 4" (10 cm) plastic pots, or use clean milk cartons
- potting soil
- water
- sunlight or a grow light

Directions:

1. Have students put potting soil into both of their plastic pots. Pat down gently.

2. Have students plant some of each kind of seed according to the package directions.

3. Water the pots.

4. Place pots in a sunny location.

5. Make sure students keep soil damp until the plants sprout.

6. Water as needed until plants are mature.

Harvesting the Salad

1. Gently pull the radishes out of the soil.
2. Cut or break off lettuce leaves.

Making the Salad

Materials needed for each group of four:

- paper towel
- large bowl
- four forks
- four paper plates
- salad dressing
- salad tongs
- child-safe knife
- water for cleaning vegetables

Direct students to do the following:

1. Remove radish leaves and discard.
2. Wash radishes and lettuce.
3. Dry gently.
4. Slice radishes, removing stem and root ends.
5. Tear lettuce leaves into bite-size pieces.
6. Place radish slices and lettuce into a bowl.
7. Toss with salad dressing.
8. Divide the salad among the group.
9. Eat and enjoy!

Homework Ideas

 • Make a list of all the different food products you can think of which are made from milk. Write your list in alphabetical order.

 • Read a story about someone who lives on a farm.

 • Go to the supermarket with a parent. Look in the produce department. Write down the names of some of the fruits and vegetables that you see. Try to find out where the fruits and vegetables were grown. (Hint: Look at the labels, packaging, or boxes. Ask the produce manager.)

 • What is your favorite food? Find out where and how it is produced. Draw a map showing how that food gets from the farm to your table.

 • Make a cow puppet from an old sock or a paper lunch bag. Create a song or skit that explains how dairy products are made. Practice your presentation in front of your family so that you will be ready to share it with the class.

 • Create a poster advertising your favorite food that comes directly from a farm. Be sure to include some facts about the food. Use words and pictures that will make the viewer want to try some!

 • How many products can you find in your home that have corn as an ingredient? Make a list.

 • Help an adult prepare something to eat using a recipe. Look at all of the ingredients in the recipe. Where did each of them come from? How were they produced? Copy the recipe and bring it in to share with the class.

Farm Fun Day

Culminate your unit of study on food from the farm to the table by having a "Farm Fun Day." Encourage students to come to school dressed as farmers. Ahead of time, make the farmer hats described on page 11 and have a few bandanas on hand to make sure that everyone has some sort of costume. Have students invite parents or another class to come and see what they have learned. Display examples of students' work in the classroom. Give a performance including the play, songs, and poems from this unit.

Send home the letter below, asking all students bring in a food to share. Serve the food on red checkered tablecloths, picnic style, on a grassy outdoor area if possible.

Award all the "farmers" in your classroom with the culminating certificates on the following page. You might wish to staple a small packet of seeds to the certificate for each student to take home and plant. (Often, local nurseries can be persuaded to donate or sell at discount to teachers.)

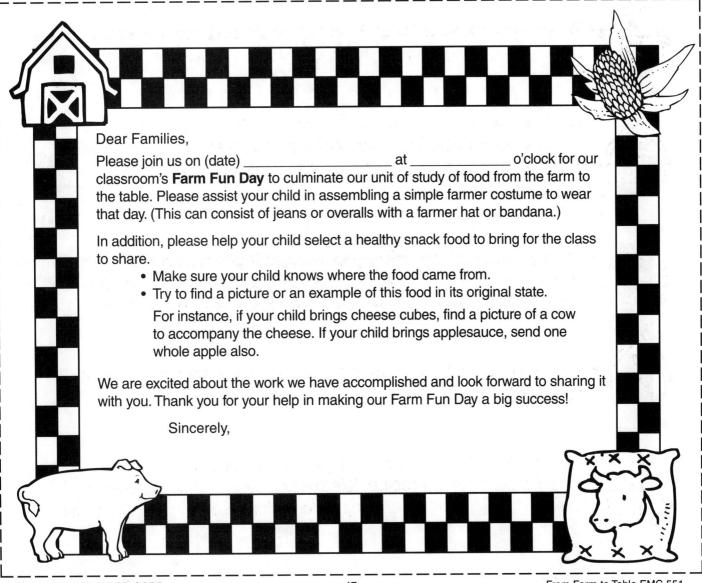

Dear Families,

Please join us on (date) _____ at _____ o'clock for our classroom's **Farm Fun Day** to culminate our unit of study of food from the farm to the table. Please assist your child in assembling a simple farmer costume to wear that day. (This can consist of jeans or overalls with a farmer hat or bandana.)

In addition, please help your child select a healthy snack food to bring for the class to share.

- Make sure your child knows where the food came from.
- Try to find a picture or an example of this food in its original state.

    For instance, if your child brings cheese cubes, find a picture of a cow to accompany the cheese. If your child brings applesauce, send one whole apple also.

We are excited about the work we have accomplished and look forward to sharing it with you. Thank you for your help in making our Farm Fun Day a big success!

    Sincerely,

 From Farm to Table EMC 551

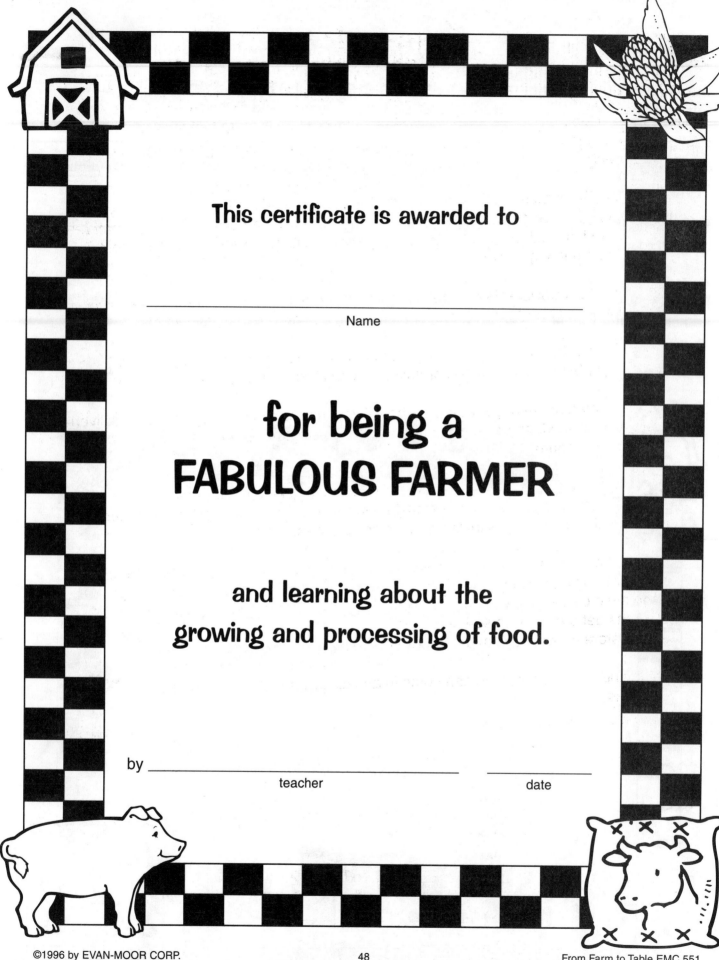

This certificate is awarded to

_____
Name

for being a
FABULOUS FARMER

and learning about the
growing and processing of food.

by _____ _____
teacher   date

48   From Farm to Table EMC 551